Passport

Passport

Richie McCaffery

Nine
Arches
Press

Passport
Richie McCaffery

ISBN: 978-1-911027-43-0

Cover artwork: Léon Spilliaert: 'La digue' (inv. 10224) – bestaande digitale illustratie © Royal Museums of Fine Arts of Belgium, Brussels / photo: J. Geleyns – Art Photography

First published July 2018 by:

Nine Arches Press
Unit 14,
Sir Frank Whittle Business Centre,
Great Central Way, Rugby.
CV21 3XH
United Kingdom

www.ninearchespress.com

Printed in the United Kingdom by:
Imprint Digital

Nine Arches Press is supported using public funding by the National Lottery through Arts Council England.

Supported using public funding by
**ARTS COUNCIL
ENGLAND**

for Stef

CONTENTS

They were worried about me
so they got together
to say how much I'm loved.

There are medieval churches
out there that still manage
to fend off the rain.

It sometimes seems like
their future depends on the sale
of a few mouldering paperbacks.

What I see and what happens
are two different countries.
I must try to remember this.

Breakdown

In bonding with my father and grandfather
we always seemed to break things.

With one I chopped down trees
and the other I tinkered with machines
so they never worked again.

The foundation of our love was destruction,
although all three of us had been created.

I've no kids of my own and no intention,
so I pull myself apart without knowing
how I can be put back together.

Postcard from Ostend

Even after the planes flew over,
levelling the city,
pre-War postcards were sold
of happy children and flowerbeds.

Like people, postcard photographs
came in generations.
Copies copied from copies,
an ebbing of definition.

Bombs and developers still couldn't
change its name. But I worry if
you visit me here you might find
someone else answering to mine.

Looking for Léon Spilliaert

We're here to find the grave
of Spilliaert, the symbolist artist,
and his wife Rachel. A hard ask
since all the ten-thousand granite
tombs look exactly the same.

You go your way, I go mine
until we're lost to each other
and I give up the search for them
and start looking for you, your
red hair bobbing against the grey.

You too are nowhere to be seen
and must be looking for me.

Double Dutch

i.

In Catholic Belgium, the norm
is to have a crucifix hanging
in every classroom. Ours
is broken and lies in bits.
It looks like a gun someone
has been ordered to surrender.
No one mentions it.

I'm the one person in my class
not fleeing war or tyranny.
They accept me, even when I say
I'm only here for love. We bond
over coffees we buy each other
and the language we're slowly
making our own.

ii.

There's a cobbled path that leads
down to my Dutch language school,
its stones a Babel of coloured granites.

In class I watch a man who's just
registered for lessons try to get
through the big glass doors.

One is wide open, the other closed.
By instinct or experience
he tries the locked door first.

Brick

They say Belgians are born with a brick
in their stomachs, such is their love
of property. It's taken us until now
to have a few thousand of our own.

I've brought little to the buying
of this place, but I do have a brick.
It's deeply stamped *Radcliffe* –
the brickworks (that no longer exist)

that made the red blocks
of the 1930s semi I called home.
My rough brick won't sit flush
in these fine walls. Still, I lay it down.

Delft tile

For your birthday you visited
and I gave you an original
17th century tile of a chevalier.
I hadn't expected them to be
so expensive and hard to find.

The tile had been repaired,
but it was all I could afford;
its back smoke stained
from where it hung above
a long-dismantled fireplace.

You say you love it, wrap it
in your clothes so it survives
the flight home through blue sky
and the blueness that persists
beyond the tile's glaze.

Kongostraat

i.

When I first moved here, I thought
the little orange bricks of the houses
looked like endless rusty chains.
The windows break them
but their Flemish bond holds strong.

I'm getting panic attacks again –
sweaty, sleepless nights.
In the morning I open the curtains
and the heat of my fear
has steamed the glass unclear.

I go to the café over the road.
The waitress greets me:
Ah, Scottish – as if I'm some
old, dimly-remembered ballad
that probably doesn't end well.

ii.

Everything about our house
is protected apart from the people
who live inside; they can

be replaced, no bother.
My bare feet still find splinters
on the many-eyed pine floorboards.

We fill the rooms with our things.
Sunlight bounces off the lot
as if rejecting them.

iii.

Skips are more of a permanent feature
on our street than the houses.
Hard to think you live in a work
in progress. You'll never see it finished.

There's one across the road now –
a giant yellow dustbin filled
with rubble, floorboards, plaster
and old Art Nouveau windows,

and a tramp thigh deep in it all
rootling around for stuff of value.
I'm sure at this moment we're thinking
the same thing but for different reasons.

iv.

We live in tall, terraced houses
like chests of drawers – empty,
filled, locked or forgotten.

Babies are carried in, the dead
brought out and we remain
as if we might come in useful.

At early dusk the old sodium
street lights come on like stages
of grief, flickering with disbelief.

Soon they're surging red with anger
and later people plead beneath
them after drunken arguments.

Finally, the steady white light
of acceptance. It's somehow
comforting to know

that even if I fail the day
or it fails me, it still passes.

Ish

From Northumberland, I feel more
Scottish than English, though these
terms suggest a netherland of nearly –
always 'ish', never one or the other.

In Ghent, although I've told
my neighbours I'm from Scotland,
they have me down as Irish –
my nationality grows on a grapevine.

These things build up. My heart is
a first forever clenching and unclenching,
never quite getting its grip or letting go.
One of these days I'll wake up cold

to find my shoes and clothes gone –
I'll have walked out on myself.

Beeldenstorm

On our first visit to Ghent –
never once thinking I'd end up
living here – you told me a story
of monks in a besieged monastery.

Aggressors on all sides, save
the side facing the river.
To escape they emptied the library
of vellum and incunabula

and poured them all into
the rushing water. Eventually
the word won out and the monks
fled over a bridge of cracked spines.

When there's a rare English term
on the tip of my tongue, it's fleeing
in favour of a daily Dutch one. We've
laid down all we had to be here.

University

i. Curriculum Vitae

We were twenty or twenty-one,
drunk and stoned, camping rough,
when we took it upon ourselves,
slat by slat, to break a pallet we
found by a track in the woods.

As we jumped in the failing light
we were trying to say nothing
could pack us up and carry us off.

It was a pine plantation –
tall with trees that were pulped
into paper only a few years later
for the council's unpayable bill
that felled me.

ii. Alumnus

On the day I graduated, I met
a man who told me
he'd just paid the last
instalment for his funeral.

I walked back to campus
with his strange joy
and my sadness and a life
somewhere, somehow to be had.

I cut through a brittle wood
and made too many false turns.
I'm still wandering there.
I can't recall a word I was taught.

iii. Alma Mater

He'd bought honey
made from parsley flowers
and *parsley* in Flemish
is *peterselie*. I collected
the word like a bit of pollen.

Honey's too expensive for me
but if money was no issue
I'd like a spoonful gathered
from the wild flowers
growing on neglected graves

of the Pathfoot villagers,
the hard workers whose homes
were flattened to make way
for my old university
and three sweet years
that come back to sting me.

Ballylar, Fanad

Here's a photo of me, your favourite –
16 years old, taken through a broken sash
at the old post office, after the rains.

I look at my younger self
and he won't meet my gaze.

He glances away from the camera but can't
remember what has caught his eye –
perhaps the twisty road to the sea

that runs down out of sight and keeps
going all the way to this older me.

Spoor

for Ian Abbot 1947-1989

The people who were best
at telling me ghost stories
as a child are long dead,
the teller now the tolled.

All the children I knew,
including the one I was,
have vanished, their
bodies never found.

In the field a black dog runs
on the trail of some scent.
No-one is calling
this running hound to heel,

perhaps no-one knows
its name to say.

Marrakech

I refuse the wares of a seller
in a souk and he tells me
'Gingers have no souls' –
I reply 'Nobody has a soul'.

I was here years ago
and have changed so much
it sometimes feels like
I've been reincarnated.

Being back I worry about
meeting that nervous boy
crossing Jemaa el-Fnaa,
passport sellotaped to his chest.

I worry he might not
acknowledge me, thinking
me yet another hawker
out for his money.

I'd be wasting my time
if I did. I could never
sell this life as it is now
to my younger self.

Currency

i.

In the restaurant on our last night
the waitress tells us
of an old German couple just in
who'd tried to pay for their meal
with shillings and farthings
left over from a holiday
many decades ago.

They thought their gelt
was current as ever,
the way we all have something
we think is valid,
to be brought out
in a flourish of earnestness
and laughed out of town.

ii.

In Bank of Scotland on Byres Road
a note affixed to the hole in the wall says:
'This machine only dispenses English banknotes.'

The form the money takes is important,
regardless what you say. You could be
a millionaire and people would tug the forelock

but tell them you have it in copper pennies
in skips in your back garden and they'd turn
on their heels. It's not enough to be

or to have, they'll find other ways of dividing.
In trying to get to the truth, I've stripped
the gold plating off the nib of this pen.

Desert rose

Your first gift to me –
a desert rose you'd found
while travelling in Egypt.

It's been on my desk
through the many house moves
we've made in three countries.

Better than anything else
you could've given me –
a flower of rock

that's bloomed for millions
of years in the most
inhospitable of places.

Career change

Give up trying to teach, persuade or influence
people about culture, religion or politics.

It's much easier to simply cook for them all;
you only need a base flavour to build on –

peel and slice the onion and notice how
you put the stink of it into all of their heads.

Ghent statues

i. Jacob van Artevelde

He was the first I saw on my evening walk,
standing in the middle of the Vrijdagmarkt,
his green-bronze hand stretched out towards
England. Hard to tell if he's reaching
to grasp something or merely push it away.

ii. Lieven Bauwens

Here's the man who smuggled
an English mule-jenny
to save the Ghent textile industry
and thus put many in the workhouse.
Whether he carries the cotton sheet
out of pride or shame
is anybody's guess.

iii. De Stroppendrager

He's just an ugly, beer-bellied Gentenaar
from the Revolt of 1540. In punishment
he walked the streets with a noose round his neck.
Now he's a symbol of city pride and strength,
a doomed survivor. I like him the best.

Moles

Your mother wants a garden full of flowers
but hates the moles and their hillocks
that punctuate the green lawn.

She gets a man in who tears them out crying
from the turf like little velvet mandrakes –
he likes to skewer them with a pitchfork.

But the moles turn the soil, the more moles
there are, the more flowers; she can't see that.
Your mother wants you to be happy,

but only on her own terms. She once
told me this loam was the pride of Belgium
because anything could flourish in it.

Roots

after Herman de Coninck

At school it was easy. If your laces
came undone during a game of tig
you simply shouted *Skinchies!*
and the world magically stopped.

There's no such charm for adults
and going home's running away.
Our problem is the tangled
roots we can't put down

in your country or mine.
We drift around with them
like loose shoelaces, knowing
in time they'll trip us up.

Auspex

after Roland Jooris

Never usually careful, crossing the road,
carrying only my life. I am carrying
a box of eggs that will never hatch.

Our neighbour's a pigeon fancier. In Dutch
this translates as a 'milker of doves'.
My sense of home's so shaky

I can't bring myself to shoo them from
our roof, their shit looks like plaster.
But whenever I dare applaud a bird

for its song, it flies off in fright.

Little farm

i.

They built the little farm when the big farm
was broken up. Divorces put these places
on the market. Here they sow tension –

conversation might bounce back up
and smack you in the face like young
wood chopped in a rush for the stove.

There's a rotten barn that needs to be
cut away from the side of the house
before it spoils the whole structure.

The family who live here are as kept
in place as their livestock, by fences
of marriage and electricities of desire.

Someone's going to be put out to pasture.
He plays guitar in the darkened barn,
the strings tense, straying out of tune.

ii.

The most money this farm ever made
was back in the 1800s when a local
militia paid the farmer to bury ten
executed, anonymous men on his land.

Being a Christian, the farmer used
small boulders he'd gathered
from the fields as markers. Those
stones are still there by the roadside,

little grey heads that won't be bowed.

Light

I've returned home sometimes
and walked all the way
through the narrow house
so mechanically
I don't know I'm there.

Going into a gloomy room
my finger instinctively
flicks the light-switch
and I pace round the room
still in some reverie.

Then comes the thought
I need more light
and I flick the switch again.
In the dark, shocked awake
I realise it wasn't enough.

Stones

i.

Although the road doesn't go
anywhere special, a man is on
his knees as if in prayer,
putting in new cobblestones.

I watch him for a minute
and one of the granite blocks
breaks under his hammer.
It won't yield to the will

of anyone or anything
other than itself, would
rather shatter than be beaten
into a place far from its quarry.

ii. Derick John Milburn (1954-1997)

A 'demonstrator' gravestone
for an undertakers
that went out of business
like the town pledged to stop dying.

They were chucking it in a skip
and I took pity, planting it
at the foot of a tree in my garden.

I can't tell what's worse:
mourning a man who never existed
or mourning the life of someone
real who never really lived.

Obituaries

i.

I read his obituary countless times,
taking it to bed, sitting upright till dawn.

I was trying to find just one typo because
that might mean a letter to the editor, perhaps

a correction, revision or even a whole-hogging
retraction of the event itself, like the loophole

I imagine he was searching for in a book he
left half-finished on his death-bed, reading

a word each night, hoping that as long as
there was a story, he'd be spared to finish it.

ii.

His wife a decade dead,
the cartilage gone out of his athlete's knees,
he existed on watery whisky, never left his bed.

I sat beside him once and he came to –
Fuck! Still here... was all he said.
I wasn't sure if he meant him or me.

iii.

On the way up Dumyat
I saw a huddled group
on the peak scattering ashes.

They made a toast
and began their descent
as I reached them.

In the stubbly heather
I found the cheap urn,
left as if they could just

abandon death on the top
of a high hill and it
would stay there.

Robin Hood's Bay

i.

He knew he was dying
when he came on holiday
like he'd done for forty years.

All I wanted to find was my
own fossil and we scoured
the beach as quickly as we could

before the tide came back in.
We found only the one –
a small, perfect ammonite.

It broke open with flakes
and nuggets of gold pyrites
like bits of sleep

in the eye of millions
and millions of years.

ii.

The palm-reader by Whitby harbour
had a plywood shed for a parlour
with a hand-painted sign:
She is nown for her truthfull predictions.

He knew his prognosis when he went in
for a reading that predicted a long life.
He'd be dead by next summer
and her business would be booming.

Echo

The night before I left
my mother drank herself silly.
I had to put her to bed.

In doing so she made sure
the roles were symbolically switched.
I was sober for once and in control.

She cried out for me twice
in the night, my name
echoing briefly in the hall.

Did she know I am the echo
that keeps coming back
saying the same thing

but each time more quietly?
I was once on a mountain
my words reverberating like a god.

Belgium is a flat land
but it feels like I'm still descending
yet to hit the bottom.

Apple

The flesh of the fruit tastes sweeter
the closer to the stem you get
but the stem itself is inedible.

I'm thinking of that apple my mother
gave me when she saw us off back
to Belgium after Christmas with her.

The seeds like little treen tears.
I spoke platitudes with her
and felt a second lump in my throat.
I threw the core in the nearest bin.

Proof-reader

My problem is I only want to read
the mutilated texts used to pad
the spines of finely bound tomes
and I want to be paid solely
with the loose change an upholsterer
gathered from decades of old chairs.

I work as a proof-reader
and make below the breadline
spotting the typos in the work
of others. Pages become days
and I should be better by now
at seeing my own mistakes.

In better moods, I tell myself
I'm like the rare first edition
which is shown to be the right one
by virtue of all its corrigenda.
Faults are sometimes more winning
and memorable than the norm –

that blackbird I loved at Stirling
for its one white tail-feather, an inky
nib rail-roading on white paper.
Where I live now, the golden mean
is demanded by law. Each night
the street is pitch-dark, no lights

on in our neighbour's homes – so sure
are they of their path they don't need
it illuminated. With my light on they
see me, I can't see them. They think
I'm the mistake in the sentence
of the street but they're skim-reading.

Spanish guitar

When your childhood home was emptied,
you gave it to me. They're usually cheap
but this one's a cut above, mellow and rich.
You could say it's the wood and craftsmanship

but it's also the hole at the centre of it,
the absence, the dead air sent singing –
melody only becomes such when it leaves
the instrument, fans out and haunts us.

It reminds me of that nature show we saw,
how tigers communicate through marked trees
and sometimes never meet, how we're just
brushing with hope against wood or paper.

Janus

My past is the back garden
at my parents' house – I've planted
more dead pets than seeds, taken
much more than's been given back
and am now scared to dig in case
I unearth something
that should be forgotten.

The seat at my desk is an old
piano stool as if I'm improvising
this life, the score's right under
my arse but I refuse to face
its music. All I know, not much,
is happiness only comes when
I forget about myself.

Present tense

I drift around the village pubs
like a soldier on leave from himself.

I'm fighting with the present tense –
I've never felt at ease in it.

I see sparrow fledglings on a wall
flapping their little tambour wings

as if they're trying to shake off
the life they've been shackled with.

The gifts

i.

It's in my blood to become
someone else in anger.

As a kid I lived in terror of Dad losing it
and the one time I did too, years later,
you wouldn't speak to me for days.

Years ago grandfather caught a burglar
red-handed and raged at him so much
the family dog attacked its owner instead.

ii.

Up to my knees in goose-shit,
I try to remember anything
you said to me years ago.

You were no miser of wisdom
but all I can remember are these words:
It's something we do well.

I know you meant the men
in our family, but the details
of our gift have gone with you.

On days like these, I settle for knowing
I have it. Others, I count myself lucky
I don't know what it is.

Calling

At Widdrington Station there's a huge railway sign
that says *London 300 miles*. It can't see the place
it points to and it can't move in its direction.

I think this is what faith is, or else a slanty fence
post that needs a hard, sharp knock on the head
to make it stand firm and upright again.

I'm still waiting on the platform for my calling
but I'm thirty and they're announcing delays.
I close my eyes and see my destination.

Ghent

Set out from Ghent
though I thanke God for it, I do hate this towne.
Hugo Claus, from *The Sign of the Hamster*

Ghent, once the big city of textiles
is where my life began
to come apart and fray.

It's also the city of good news –
I work in an archive with newspapers
but nothing ever happens to me.

At the end of the day my fingers
are black like I'm a mechanic of words
tinkering with something I can't fix.

Once I woke early, in the dark,
and pulled a black jumper over my head
and I still seem to be pulling.

Who's to say that when my mood
plummets, it's not like the crow
swooping down for something it's seen.

That crow's plumage, too, is often
so black it seems to my eyes blue –
despair softening to melancholy.

Ghent is also a city of boats and canals
but it takes a dirty little dinghy
to reach the best yachts in the harbour.

Typical me

to see the sculptures
and imagine marble dust scarring
the lungs of the sculptor.

I once found a sovereign by the river –
must've been a month's wages
for someone over a century ago.

It wasn't good luck, more a curse.
Spent so many fruitless days
looking for others, I ended up paying.

These times call for faith like the broken
bottle necks you find on the beach,
vulcanite stoppers still holding strong.

Baudelopark

The days pass by and rarely
make eye contact with me.

Art Nouveau townhouses are knocked
down and styleless flats rise in their place.

If I sit on this bench long enough
someone might make a project of me.

Pigeons peck at a stale mattentaart
like they're sculpting with hunger.

It's raining, always raining.
I stick out my tongue, it stays dry.

Everyone around me is speaking Flemish
as if my life's a TV that was switched off

suddenly and switched back on again
locked into a different channel.

There's a tree branch in the wind knocking
against someone's window, like one

of those tedious people you get at parties
who flick glasses to see if they're crystal.

I'm waiting for the tree's verdict:
is this all for real?

The paper cut

On my tour today of the old bookshops
I saw a man trying to sell an outdated set

of encyclopaedias – ten volumes he had
in a sack, turned down by each bookseller.

Our bodies are like that, a sack for definitions
outdated almost as soon as they see print.

I'm glad of this paper cut – it hurts. Reminds
me of something the doctor said to Dad

how if you notice a change for the worse
and don't feel any pain, you're done for.

Iconography

i. Daily bread

In the toilet of a local church
there's an antique enamel bread bin
serving as a basket for used paper towels
after all of the flock have washed
their hands of God for another week.

It's an example of how far things
can be taken out of their context
and people still don't even notice.
They've taken Christ out of his body
and the body out of Christ.

ii. St. Jacob's, Ghent

A bird had nested on the nape
and shoulders of a bronze statue
of crucified Jesus.

While his thorny head lolled
to the side you could hear the chicks
singing for their supper.

I'm becoming surer and surer
the only life worth having
is the one that thrives

in the unintended crevices
of a received story.

iii. The ark

From the raised beach of the loft
a Victorian wooden ark with carved
animals covered in lead paint.

The whole menagerie's there
but the children who played with it
have not been spared the flood.

Oil and blood

I find oil spilled in place of blood –
doorsteps, confessional booths, sinks.
And blood where there should be oil,
under cars after road rage, in heating bills,
pooling around the midnight lamps.

The machines bleed and we merely leak,
or rather we've engineered new ways
of suffering and hurt that make the old
ones mechanical. Shed blood still tries
to clot as if it's part of the healing process.

His old tools rusted away in the shed.
An outsider might think this was because
his life was perfect, needed no repair,
but they'd be much mistaken.

Nowhere

I want to write something that will be
more important than any official document
relating to me. I live in a maze of symbols,
always in two places at once.

Droppings from the house martin nest
fall like wax from a blazing candle,
the branches of a tree look like a bundle
of walking sticks searching for *terra firma*.

I pull unsavoury thoughts from my head
like stranger's stray hair found in food.
A crumpled up rejected poem on paper
unfurls in the bin like it's flowering.

There were doves in the street before
and naturally I thought of peace
but a car back-fired and they were off –
that's where symbols get us.

Postcard

Years after your death I twig
you only bought me fountain pens
because you expected me to go
and write home from abroad.

Dad's on holiday but he's more away
when he's here and I keep moving
like my life's a magic trick
the conjurer isn't sure how to end.

We caught a hearse loggerheads
on a small sandy track on Harris.
Reversing in the face of death,
we never expected it to back down.

All I know is I don't want to end up
like the tripod chairs that lurked
in your house, as if they'd gnawed
off a fourth leg trying to escape.

Bottle show

In the Masonic hall of an ex-mining town,
hit hard so many times in the past
it toyed with the idea of staying down,

bottle diggers get together to peddle
their finds from a discarded past –
treasures once deemed rubbish.

What gets me is their language, a rich
lexicon: glass is never 'light green'
but *aqua*, iridescence is *bloom*.

When value is taken away, we
will always find new ways to worth.

Resolution

Out shopping in the street,
he fell on top of his shadow
and it vanished.

*

People I love are dying off
as if to make room for
something that isn't there.

*

You could hurt me most
of all, yet I give myself
without stint.

*

We are still here, where
nothing is as close or far
as our next breaths.

Eye test

There came a point,
after shining the light
right in my eyes,

that all I could see
was cracked clay,
like a dried-up lake.

The optician explained
this was inside my eye
and it was healthy.

In bed that night
I looked in your eyes
and you into mine.

I recalled the crazing,
how gaze is a drought
and that's as it should be.

Day in the life

I spend my days in the library researching
dead poets. I order up their manuscripts
and try to decipher them, typing up
my finds later at the dining table
to reflect the meal I've made of my life.
I'm a document being forever revised.

The library is zealously policed – pencil only
so you can't leave a permanent mark.
Anything you do leave will be erased.
Once my day is over you wait for me
outside the library. Outside all investigation,
scrutiny and rational explanation.

Balancing the books

i.

In second-hand bookshops in England
the price is pencilled in the front
of the book, but here in Belgium
it lurks on the rear end-paper.
One wants you to buy the story
on faith, the other on inspection.

ii.

My mother made the shelves for me
when I was little, from old doors sawn in two.

When she put them up, she knocked on walls
as if someone behind might answer.

I write this facing books and behind them
more books and behind them bricks

and behind it all, time and distance,
there she is, knocking
on the other side of the wall.

iii.

I'm spending too much of my life
in old bookshops.

They're places displaced stories
are just trying to find their way –
giving it one last go,
hanging onto a fragile belief
in their own residual relevance.

I take a book off the shelf
and splay its pages
like a pigeon-fancier with
a prize bird, knowing fine well
it might never make it home.

The dippers

Cinclus cinclus

On the way to your lecture, we spotted
a dipper couple on the banks of the Kelvin,
so immersed in themselves and their
two elements of land and river. We were
between two places, in Glasgow
for a month then back to Belgium,
our lives holding breath under water.

They made our day, those dippers, though
they never saw us from the bridge. As we
kissed each other goodbye, we too thought
we were unseen, but a colleague of yours
said they'd never witnessed an act
more loving. If we please ourselves first
we stand the best chance of pleasing others.

Spring-cleaning

Yesterday my sister gave birth
to a boy. Today I spruced up
the house for their arrival.

A light-bulb in the living-room
had popped, I replaced it
standing on a phonebook.

Ten thousand names raised me
only a couple of inches.
That was enough.

Ballast

You complain about your size
and I'm never happy about mine.
Even if we're thinner since coming here
we'll still have put on weight
in ways that don't show on scales.

I never entered into this lightly.
The thing is, I need your weight
right now, and you need mine –
all of it, as ballast to stop
the whole thing from capsizing.

Left hand drive

Saw his old car yesterday
parked on the Dampoortstraat.

Not his exactly, but the same
colour, model and year.

Wanted so badly for him
to live again and this to be

his car to pick me up in
from school and its bullies.

The car was empty and when
I looked in, the steering wheel

was set where I used to sit
as if I'm now expected to drive.

Corner

One thing my father told me
in appreciating old buildings
was that once upon a time
architects celebrated corners.

Where streets traded names
and the wind turned political –
pro or anti in your face –
the prettiest houses stood.

If he could have afforded
to choose, he'd have lived
on the corners of streets
in towns unfallen from grace.

Today I'm turning a corner,
its house has curved windows,
the stone is solid and rounded
and something to behold.

An endangered bird made its nest
in the middle of my poem
and I can't carry on, but
I can't abandon it either.

after Marcus Cumberlege

Acknowledgements and Thanks

Thank you to the magazines and online journals where some of these poems have previously featured: *Agenda, Ambit, Antiphon, Butcher's Dog, Causeway / Cabhsair, The Compass, Cyphers, The Dark Horse, The Enchanting Verses, English: The Journal of the English Association, Fras, The Frogmore Papers, Gutter, The Interpreter's House, Lighthouse, Magma, New Walk, The Next Review, The North, Northwords Now, Oxford Poetry, The Poet's Republic, The Rialto, Sarasvati, Snakeskin, Southbank Poetry, Stand, Under the Radar* and *Versopolis*.

The coda poem, '*An endangered bird made its nest*', is written after a poem by Marcus Cumberlege from his 2014 book *Haiku: Mod and Trad* (The Paper Tiger, Bruges).

Richie McCaffery would like to thank:
Stefanie Van de Peer, Jane Commane, Chris Powici, Matthew Stewart, Paul Stephenson, Vicki Feaver, Jackie McCaffery, Will Stone, and the late Alexander Hutchison.